CONTENTS

THE CASTLE

THE HUGE, STONE WALLS of the castle rise up like cliffs above the waters of the moat. The castle presents a blank, silent face to the outside world. But inside the walls, there is a completely different world. Hundreds of people live there and they all lead busy lives. They all work for the lord of the castle and, like bees in a hive, they each have their special jobs to do.

The remains of once proud castles lie scattered across Europe and the Middle East. They were built during the Middle Ages, a period which lasted from about AD 1000 to 1500. In times of war, their strong walls gave shelter against attacking armies. But castles were also the homes of kings, princes and powerful lords. So many people helped to run a castle and its lands that it could sometimes look like a small town.

△ Leeds Castle in Kent, England, dates back to the eleventh century. After it came into the king's hands in 1278, it was rebuilt and used as a royal palace for 300 years.

▷ This cutaway picture shows the chambers inside Scarborough Castle, England, as they looked in the twelfth century.

A writer described a French family's castle in 1117: 'Above were dwelling rooms and the great chamber in which the lord and his wife slept ... In the upper storey were garret rooms, in which on one side the sons slept, on the other, the daughters ... Stairs led from house to *loggia* where they used to sit in conversation.'

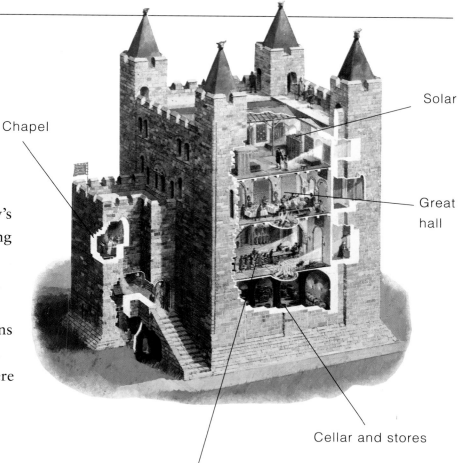

Chapel

Solar

Great hall

Cellar and stores

Treasury

People in the Middle Ages were organized into ranks. At the top was the king. Then came lords and nobles. At the bottom were the peasants. This system was at the heart of castle life.

FEUDALISM

The picture on the left shows peasants in France farming land around the castle. They gave part of their produce to the lord, and in return received land and protection. The lord received his land from the king, and in return promised to fight for him. This system is known as feudalism.

THE LORD'S VISIT

GATEHOUSE

A KNIGHT AND HIS LADY ride into their castle in the Middle East. Their arrival has taken the castle servants by surprise. A farm worker saw them and came running to tell the steward. The steward welcomes them at the gatehouse and orders the servants to bring food and wine for the tired travellers.

△ A knight and his lady arrive at a castle in the Middle East.

In 1095, the Pope called on Europe's Christian knights to make a 'crusade', to capture the holy city of Jerusalem from its Muslim rulers. Some of these crusaders settled in the Middle East and took over Muslim castles. Their new estates worked like those in Europe. Local peasants worked on the farms of their new lords, and paid them taxes.

▷ Rich ladies sometimes travelled in covered chairs carried between two horses.

Rich and powerful lords might own several castles. They would spend about a month in one and then move on to the next. Travel at this time was very slow and uncomfortable as the roads were so bad. Bandits attacked and robbed travellers, so people journeyed in groups.

SUGAR FROM THE EAST

Knights travelled between castles across Europe and the Middle East. Some knights, belonging to a group called the Order of St John, used a castle at Kolossi in Cyprus. A sugar mill, shown here, was built there. Sugar was one of many delicacies brought back to Europe by the crusaders. Sugar would have been a welcome luxury at castle feasts.

TREASURY

The lord calls a meeting in the treasury to deal with castle business. He sits on a raised platform at one end and people are brought in to speak to him. A peasant asks permission to leave the estate. A writer presents his book as a gift. In the doorway, a nobleman from a neighbouring castle arrives with his attendants, to propose a marriage between his son and the lord's daughter.

The castle was the business centre and bank for the whole region. People brought gifts to the lord. Peasants paid their taxes, in the form of produce as well as money. Cows, pigs, sheep, chickens, vegetables, eggs and butter were herded and carried into barns on the castle estate. A person called the bailiff looked after the land and collected these tributes.

△ The Duke of Berry, a powerful French noble, is presented with a book by its author.

GREAT LORDS

Castle estates made some lords so rich and powerful that even the king could not control them. John of Gaunt, Duke of Lancaster, shown above, received about £10,000 from his estates in 1394-5. One of his servants would have received about £3 a year. The lord paid the knights who fought for him about £20 a year each. He also gave them valuable gifts to keep these dangerous men content in his service.

The steward was the most important person in the castle after the lord. He was in charge of everything when the lord was away. The servants inside the castle and the farmers outside its walls all answered to him. He was in charge of the treasury, looking after the accounts and checking the farmers' taxes.

▽ Important documents were sealed with a lord's coat of arms, like this royal German seal of 1376.

The lord did not sign documents, but sealed them in wax with his coat of arms to show that they came from him. In a French document sealed in 1245 were the words: 'To all those who shall see these letters, we whose seals are attached to this present writing make known that we ... have pledged and bound ourselves and our heirs [always] to help each other.'

A FAMILY HOME

SOLAR

AFTER A TIRING DAY, the lord's family move to their private living room, called the solar. The steward waits to discuss important matters with the lord. Outside, the night is cold and wet but the family are kept warm by a large log fire. They are surrounded by comfortable furniture and beautiful tapestries. Many of the furnishings were brought with them from their other castle.

△ In the solar, the lord studies documents, the lady paints and their children play with toy knights. The steward waits to discuss business matters.

Most families lived crowded together in small rooms, but the lord's family had large, private chambers. The solar at the top of the castle allowed them peace and quiet away from the busy castle. Windows were fitted with painted glass, and the floor was scattered with sweet-smelling herbs. At Windsor Castle, near London, the walls were painted green with gold stars. In Italy, Emperor Frederick II lived in amazing castle chambers, with painted ceilings and floors of gold.

COMFORTABLE BEDS

Beds were the largest and most expensive pieces of castle furniture. Curtains were hung round this German couple's bed to keep out draughts. In her will of 1360, one noble lady left this item:

'My bed of green velvet with red stripes, the coverlet of white fur and the room-hangings patterned with parrots and blue cockerels.'

Even the richest castles did not have that much furniture. There were a few wooden chairs and tables in the solar, and beds in the bedchambers. Clothes and other belongings were stored in large, wooden chests.

◁ Tapestries like this one were hung on cold castle walls to bring colour and warmth to the rooms.

LADY'S BEDCHAMBER

The lady of the castle admires the new decorations of her private bedchamber. It is furnished even more beautifully than the other private rooms. The lady spends much of her time here, planning a busy day ahead. She comes here also to sew, and to gossip with her ladies-in-waiting. The lord and his friends can enter by invitation only.

Wealthy lords visited neighbouring castles to arrange for their daughters to marry the sons of powerful families. Through such a marriage, a lady could become very important. If her husband was away fighting, she might take over the affairs of his castle from the steward. If her husband was killed in battle, she might run the castle herself, or influence her sons when they became lords.

△ The lady's bedchamber in Leeds Castle, England. The walls are decorated with rich hangings.

◁ A portrait of a rich lady, painted in 1480.

If she did not obey her husband, a woman might be beaten. A priest in the thirteenth century wrote: 'A man may chastise his wife and beat her for correction, for she is of his household, therefore the lord may chastise his own.' But even in medieval times, some women held different views. In a poem called *The Canterbury Tales*, a woman called the Wife of Bath remembers how she beat her three husbands: 'O Lord! The pain I did them and the wo.'

A WOMAN'S WORK

A lady's duties in a French castle were described in the 1300s:

'She must know how much money comes from the estates and arrange to live without debts ... She will make sure her workers are not lazy.'

A lord's wife had several ladies-in-waiting, like the ones shown here in her bedchamber. They cleaned her rooms and wove clothes for the castle community. The lady's senior lady-in-waiting was often one of her relatives.

SCHOOLROOM

The castle priest gives the lord and lady's young children their daily lessons. One boy is trying hard to learn Latin, but he finds it difficult to concentrate. His sisters are having much more fun, listening to a lute player as they are taught to dance.

A thirteenth-century poem listed the manners a child should be taught: 'A good child upright he must stand, Before his lord when he doth eat, Nor scratch his limbs with either hand, And if a great gift or small is given, While kneeling he must render thanks.'

◁ This wooden cradle was used in the fifteenth century.

Many lords and ladies saw little of their young children. Soon after birth, babies were taken away to be looked after by wet-nurses. When they were older, children were taught Latin by the castle priest. Boys trained to become knights. Girls learnt to be ladies.

◁ Children in the castle schoolroom learnt to read and write, and to dance.

YOUNG LOVE

Royal marriages were an important way of linking countries together to make them more powerful. In 1160, the King of France's daughter was only three years old when she was married to the King of England's son. He was five! Rings, like these fourteenth-century examples set with sapphires, were exchanged as tokens of loyalty between husband and wife.

THE CHAPEL

IN THE CASTLE CHAPEL, a knight kneels before the altar. Tomorrow, he will fight for the king against his enemies. Apart from the sound of his prayers, all around him is silence. The bright morning sunlight streams in through the beautiful stained-glass windows, throwing colourful patterns on to the floor.

LESSONS IN PICTURES

Many people could not read at this time, so paintings on the chapel windows and walls told them stories from the Bible. A peasant described the wall of a chapel in France:

'I see painted pictures of Heaven and Hell, where the damned are burned. The one makes me happy, while the other makes me frightened.'

△ This chapel window in the Netherlands shows a knight praying for success in battle.

Religion played a very important part in castle life. Most people went to church at least once a week. The lord and his family attended daily services in the castle chapel. In early castles, the chapel was a small, simple room in the keep. But later, much bigger chapels were built, with stone statues and windows of coloured glass.

◁ St John's Chapel, in the Tower of London. This was a royal chapel inside the keep, and the walls were once covered with paintings.

WORDS OF WISDOM

Priests and clerks looked after the written documents in a castle. Much of what we know today about the Middle Ages comes from their records. Monks, like the one shown above, decorated books with beautiful pictures called 'illuminations'.

The Christian Church was the biggest landowner in Europe, and owned many castles. Some bishops were as rich and powerful as the greatest lords. It was written of Bishop Odo of Bayeux, in France: 'He was the foremost man after the king. He was master of the land when the king was in Normandy. He built many castles throughout the land.'

HEALTH AND HYGIENE

GARDEN

Two young nobles sit with one of the castle's many dogs in the lord's private garden. It lies hidden behind high stone walls. Small paths lead between the flower beds, and the air is full of the smell of lavender and roses. The only sounds to break the silence are the cooing from the castle dovecotes and the humming of bees around their hives.

△ Lovers in a castle garden in 1435.

△ Bees were kept for their honey and wax.

Many castles had gardens tucked away behind their strong walls. Records show that in 1283, turf was transported by river to lay a lawn during the building of Conway Castle in Wales. A squire was paid three pence to water it. Castle gardens contained fishponds, fountains, fruit trees, vines, and flower beds planted with roses, lilies and herbs. For strolling lovers, there were seats hidden by flowers, called 'roosting places'.

PLANT YOUR OWN HERB GARDEN

The castle herb garden was divided into equal sections. Divide a plot of earth into four small squares with gravel paths between them.

In the squares you can plant the following herbs:
– **Sage**, used in tea to relieve headaches and colds, and as a hair rinse.
– **Rosemary**, used as a shampoo, to leave hair scented and shiny.
– **Lavender**, used in perfumes.
– **Thyme**, used in pot-pourris and medicines. Oil from thyme is still used as an antiseptic.

YOU WILL NEED
Gravel
A trowel
Sage, Rosemary, Lavender, Thyme

Doctors treated their patients using herbs from the castle garden. Their healing powers were listed in books called 'herbals'. The best of these were written by Arabic doctors. In the eleventh century, a Persian called Avicenna wrote a book called the *Canon of Medicine*, which was over one million words long. It was translated into Latin and became one of the most important medical books in Europe.

◁ This picture comes from an Italian version of a herbal written in the Middle East.

GARDEROBE

Peter the gongfermor inspects the castle toilets. He performs many tasks around the castle, mostly clearing away rubbish and cleaning out the moat. Once a week, he has to clean the toilet pits. It is dirty, smelly work, but somebody has to do it. Most of the people in the castle keep away from him. But he is perfectly happy, because his wife loves him.

Toilets were built into the castle's outer walls, in small rooms called *garderobes*. People believed that the smell from toilets protected clothes from moths and bugs. This is why the toilet was called a garderobe. It comes from the French *garder* (to keep) and *robe* (dress). The toilets emptied straight into the moat, or into pits which were emptied by cleaners called gongfermors.

△ The garderobes at Langley Castle, in England, each had their own private cubicles.

CASTLE CURES

If people in the castle fell ill, doctors treated them by bleeding. This tended to make patients feel even worse than before. Doctors made medicines from mixtures of herbs, spices, and even powdered metals and insects. Honey mixed with herbs was used to treat sore throats and upset stomachs. For toothache, patients were given a mixture of vinegar, oil and sulphur to apply to the mouth.

In 1365, King Edward III of England complained that the area round Lincoln Castle was filthy: 'He therefore urges that the streets and lanes be cleaned up at once.' A castle was swept from top to bottom once or twice a year, when the lord's family were away. But it soon became dirty again. People did not take baths very often. The lice and fleas that lived in their hair and clothes could quickly spread diseases from person to person.

▷ Armed with a bucket and spade, the gongfermor sets about his work.

SERVANTS

STABLES

Ｏｎ ａ ｃｏｌｄ, ｃｒｉｓｐ ＭＯＲＮＩＮＧ the grooms start work in the stables. The clip-clop of horses' hooves echoes across the courtyard as they are led out for their daily exercise. One team are hitched up to a grand carriage, as a group of royal ladies prepare to travel. Other, much larger horses are prepared for the lord and his knights to ride into battle.

'The Queen and her ladies travelled in covered litters with a large escort of noblemen. The litters were richly decorated. The horses drawing them went at walking pace.' This description of the Queen of France's transport was written in 1389. Carriages and horses were kept in the castle stables, and were looked after by the grooms. The grooms were under the command of the marshal. He was also in charge of the soldiers who defended the castle and all the servants who worked outside. These included the carpenters and stonemasons who kept the castle in good repair.

△ Although carriages could look beautiful, they were not very comfortable inside.

◁ Castelnau was built in France in the twelfth century. Its inhabitants had to pay a rent of one egg per year.

BADGES OF OFFICE

Castle servants wore the coat of arms of their master. Senior officials wore silver chains of office, while lesser servants had cloth badges stitched to their jackets. This coat of arms of a German knight shows how women sometimes play tricks on men.

▷ Blacksmiths worked in larger castles making arrowheads, mending armour and forging iron shoes for the stable's horses.

Horses were not the only beasts of burden in the castle. Oxen were used to pull ploughs and wagons. In France, once a year, four oxen drew a wagon from Castelnau castle to the lands of the count who ruled the region. The wagon was loaded with a single egg. The king had ordered the occupants of Castelnau to pay the count one egg each year, as rent for their castle.

WINDMILL

The huge sails creak slowly round on a windmill built high up on the castle walls. The miller and his two assistants drag heavy sacks across the wooden floors, and empty the grain on to the millstones. The flour from the crushed grain pours into large sacks and another assistant carries these off to the castle kitchen. The flour will be made into loaves of piping-hot bread.

△ Dover Castle. The manuscript picture beneath it shows a miller and his mill.

Some castles had their own windmill or watermill. Peasants had to pay the miller to grind their grain into flour, so he was often disliked. Dover Castle, in England, had a windmill on one of its towers, and a well sunk ninety metres into the cliffs beneath it. These provided food and drink for the castle community when they were besieged by enemy forces.

A garrison of soldiers was kept at a castle whenever there was danger of attack. In times of peace, only a few men were on duty to guard the lord's property. They were recruited from surrounding villages and towns. The castle servants were responsible for keeping these soldiers housed and fed. If they were well looked after, they were less likely to turn against their lord.

△ An armourer making a coat of chain mail.

MASTERS OF METAL

Whole villages in Italy and Germany specialized in making armour. Each stage was done by different craftsmen. Hammerers and polishers made plates of steel. A locksmith joined them together with hinges. A master armourer made helmets, which were decorated by engravers.

A mailmaker worked in the castle armoury, making chain mail for the castle's soldiers. First, he cut pieces of wire, and bent them around a tiny anvil. He then linked thousands of these rings together with tiny rivets to form a coat of chain mail. A whole coat could take weeks to complete.

COURTYARD

It is market day. Knights, peasants, pedlars, priests and beggars all mingle together in the castle courtyard. Merchants display rich silks, precious stones and spices from lands to the east, and gold and furs from the north. Farmers have brought fruit and vegetables and live animals to sell. They barter with craftsmen for leather shoes, pots and pans and candles. Children gather round the many jugglers and musicians.

◁ At the weekly market, merchants trade goods and discuss business. Outside the castle gates people sell food to the shoppers.

MARKET GOODS

A writer described the goods on sale in a market in France in the fourteenth century:

'There were few women who did not have something from overseas towns: clothing, furs, bedcovers, cutlery ... tablecloths and linen, bowls in wood and silver.'

THE FUN OF THE FAIR

Fairs were held once or twice a year. They were much bigger than the weekly markets, and brought traders from far and wide. At these fairs, masked actors known as 'mummers' (left) performed short plays. These were very noisy and bloodthirsty. Any characters who 'died' during the play were brought back to life at the end by a doctor. You can see him wearing a mask at the top.

The castle community depended on the surrounding peasants to bring food to market, as well as the leather and wool they needed to make shoes and clothes. But as well as being a centre of trade, a castle also acted as a refuge in times of war. If enemies approached, the farmers and villagers living outside the castle could find safety behind its strong walls.

▷ The massive walls of Avila, in Spain. Perched on a hill, the town was a centre of trade and place of safety for the surrounding area.

WEAVING ROOM

The women of the household gather in the weaving room. The lord's wife sits in the centre surrounded by her ladies-in-waiting. Some of them are using cards to untangle the fibres of wool. Others use spindles to spin the fibres into thread. They all chatter and laugh as they work.

◁ Women spinning and weaving.

Most of the castle servants were male. The few women servants worked in the laundry and kept the lady's chambers stocked with clean linen, candles and bowls of hot water for washing in the mornings. Women also made clothes for everyone in the castle. They washed and combed raw wool, then spun it into thread. This was woven into cloth on looms and made into clothing.

PICTURES IN WOOL

Tapestries show us the sorts of clothes people wore in the castle. Peasants had simple woollen garments in plain colours. Rich people wore colourful silk from the Middle East, and velvet trimmed with fur. These nobles are dressed for a bear hunt.

WEAVE YOUR OWN TAPESTRY

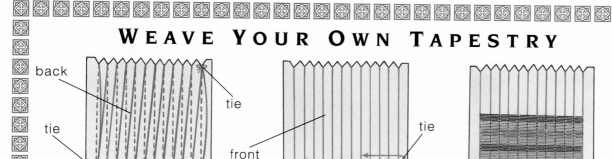

back

tie

tie

front

tie

tie

1. Cut teeth along the top and bottom of a piece of card. Loop a single thread of wool between the teeth furthest left. Tie a knot at the back. Thread the loose end between the remaining teeth, and knot behind the last tooth. This creates the 'warp' threads.

2. To start weaving, tie a second thread (the 'weft') to the right-hand warp thread. Next, work across, weaving the weft thread over and under. Then, work back across, this time weaving under and over the opposite warp threads.

3. Keep the weft threads pushed together. You can change the colour and pattern by tying a new weft thread on to the last one. To remove the completed tapestry, bend the card and carefully lift off the warp threads.

A French poem from the Middle Ages describes the importance of women in the castle:

> 'Much ought woman to be held dear.
> By her is everybody clothed.
> Woman spins and makes garments
> Of cloth of gold and cloth of silk.
> To all who read this story I say,
> Speak no ill of womankind.'

▷ The most senior lady-in-waiting had a comfortable room near the family's private apartments.

THE DUNGEON

THE CASTLE JAILER UNLOCKS the door to the gloomy dungeon. Prisoners sit silently in this damp, dark place. Water drips down the walls, and rats nibble at the prisoners' toes. A foreign nobleman shouts at the jailer, demanding to know why he is being imprisoned in this hell-hole with common peasants and thieves.

Some castles had dungeons built deep inside them where prisoners were kept for many years. Their only contact with the outside world was their jailer who brought them food once a day. Important prisoners captured in battle were usually held in comfortable rooms until their families paid huge ransoms to release them. Less fortunate prisoners were locked in tiny pits called *oubliettes*, a word which comes from the French for forgotten.

△ In the castle dungeon, the worst of the prisoners peers up from an oubliette.

▽ Witnesses in a
French trial of 1331.

Trials for the region round the castle took
place in the great hall. The lord himself acted as
the judge for really serious crimes, but usually
the steward was in charge. At some trials,
defendants were made to pick up red-hot iron
bars or plunge their hands into boiling water.
If the skin blistered, they were found guilty.

INSTRUMENTS OF TORTURE

A few unfortunate prisoners, such
as those accused of treason, were
taken to the torture chamber. Here,
they were made to confess to their
crimes. Their bodies were stretched
on racks until their bones broke, or
their fingers were crushed in
thumbscrews. In terrible pain, they
would often agree to say anything
that their torturers wanted to hear.

FOOD AND DRINK

KITCHEN

IMPORTANT GUESTS HAVE ARRIVED, and the kitchen buzzes with activity. A huge banquet is being prepared. The head cook barks orders, and prowls through the steam of the bubbling cauldrons and vats. He holds a large spoon in one hand, which he uses both to taste the food and to keep the kitchen staff in order!

△ The kitchen of Kreuzenstein Castle, in Austria.

In the castle kitchen, a huge fire burned all the year round, even during the hot summer months. Great joints of meat were roasted on spits over the flames. A young boy known as the 'turnspit' sat all day beside the fire turning a handle to rotate the meat. It was hot, tiring work.

Drink was stored in barrels in the castle cellar. Beer was brewed from barley or oats, and cider from apples and pears. In warm areas, grapes for wine were grown in castle vineyards. Drink was served in face-jugs like those on the left.

The kitchen was full of delicious smells. Chickens and puddings boiled in cauldrons, hung over the fire. Pots and pans bubbled with rich sauces, and thick stews and soups called 'pottages'. The scent of herbs mixed with the aroma of bread ovens.

COOKING PEASE POTTAGE

INGREDIENTS *(for six people):* 450 g dried green peas, 900ml milk, 1 teaspoon ground black pepper, 1 teaspoon salt

1. Soak the peas overnight in a bowl of cold water.

2. Drain and rinse them in fresh water.

3. Place them in a saucepan with the milk. Heat slowly, stirring regularly. Do not let the milk come to the boil.

4. When the peas are soft, remove them from the heat. Mash them into a thick cream with the milk. Add the salt and pepper and serve.

GREAT HALL

With a fanfare of trumpets, a special feast is served in the great hall. The lord and lady sit with friends at the high table, beneath the minstrels' gallery. Pages and squires serve them with gold and silver plates. These contain dishes of venison and wild boar, peacocks and herons served with their feathers on, and sweets carved in the shapes of castles.

Food was brought into the hall in a long procession led by the chief carver and cupbearer. Mutton, beef and even bear meat was served. There were birds of every size, from larks to swans. Before he began the feast by carving the meats, the chief carver held up his carving knife and solemnly kissed it.

Each course in a feast was made up of several dishes. The guests chose one or two from each. After the meat course, delicious fruit tarts and milk puddings were served. There were endless supplies of wine and beer. On special occasions, sweets called 'subtleties' were served. These were made from sugar, almond paste and jelly, modelled into fantastic shapes.

TABLE MANNERS

A book of good table manners written in the fifteenth century included this advice:

'If there is a man of God sitting at the table, take great care where you spit. Do not belch near your neighbour's face, especially if your breath is foul. Pick not your teeth at the table with knife, straw or stick.'

△ A procession of servants enters the great hall to serve the wealthy guests with their magnificent feast.

ENTERTAINMENT

LOGGIA

A LONG DRUM ROLL from the minstrels' gallery announces the lord's jester. He bursts into the chamber and begins to juggle with incredible skill. The jester wears a hat with huge ears, and a brightly coloured costume with bells which tinkle as he walks. He only has to look at the guests and they collapse into helpless laughter.

▷ The jester made a fool of himself. He also liked to make fools of the people who were laughing at him.

The lord of the castle had a jester to entertain him and his guests after the feast. The jester's jokes and songs could be very rude and he said things which no one else would have dared. Not everyone was amused by the jester. One priest wrote that the entertainers he had seen 'do change and distort their bodies with shameful leaps and gestures.'

After a feast, the lord and his knights relaxed in an open gallery called the *loggia*. Here they played chess, a game popular in Muslim and crusader castles. The castle workers also enjoyed themselves. They played a rough sport similar to football, and a form of hockey called 'bandyball'.

MUSICAL INSTRUMENTS

All sorts of musical instruments could be heard in the castle. There were droning bagpipes (right) and gentle harps; organs called hurdy-gurdies (left), played by turning a handle; little flutes and much larger pipes (below-right). In the belt of the jester on page 36 are a pipe and 'tabor' drum, which he could play at the same time. Pairs of drums called 'nakers' (left) were played to accompany dancers.

△ Two men play a ball game. Behind them, two others play chess in the loggia.

▽ This strange-looking instrument, called a gittern, was played in the thirteenth century.

The entertainments at the feasts of the Count of Foix, in France, were described by a writer in 1388: 'He took great pleasure in minstrelsy ... He liked his clerks to sing songs ... and he also enjoyed having travelling entertainers to perform between courses. After he had watched them, he sent them round the tables of the knights and squires.'

ESTATES

A thundering noise gets louder and louder, and the ground begins to tremble. A deer breaks out of the trees, closely followed by barking hounds and a group of magnificent horsemen. For a moment, they stop in a clearing beneath the castle walls. The lead horseman blows his horn, then they charge away once more across the castle estates.

The estate of a castle was spread round it like a patchwork quilt as far as the eye could see. Perched high up on a hill, the castle protected the land about it; but the land kept the castle alive. Its fields and forests supplied the castle with fuel and food.

△ The forests and fields of Chirk Castle estate in Wales as they look today.

◁ French huntsmen and their hounds kill a wild boar on their castle estate.

Hunting was one of the most popular sports for the rich. Huge areas of forest were reserved just for the king's hunt. Stags were considered the greatest catch. Wolves, bears and boar ran wild on castle estates and were all dangerous prey. One writer said of a wild boar: 'He is more formidable than any armed man.'

KINGS OF THE SKIES

This picture shows French nobles 'hawking', using birds of prey to catch smaller birds and rabbits. Hawks were extremely valuable and a lord kept his favourite hunting bird in his private castle rooms. A thirteenth-century essay explained how to train a hawk: 'You must keep him on your fist more than ever before, and take him into the law-courts and into church.'

AROUND THE WORLD

Dawn is breaking over the many sloping roofs of a castle in Japan. The Samurai warriors inside the castle are saying their prayers and putting on their elaborate leather armour. In the castle courtyard, the heavy wooden gates have been opened and farmers from the surrounding countryside are bringing in supplies on creaking wooden carts.

Japanese castles were built with strong walls to withstand attacks and earthquakes. Life in a Japanese castle was similar to that in a European one. As well as the lord and his family, a garrison of soldiers lived there. The castle served as the centre for law, trade and learning for the whole region. There were workshops inside its walls, where beautiful objects such as lacquer furniture and painted screens were made to decorate the lord's apartments.

△ White Egret Castle, at Himeji in Japan, was built in the fourteenth century.

COOL COURTYARDS

The Red Fort in Delhi, India, was completed during the reign of an emperor called Shah Jahan (1628-1666). Behind its powerful red stone walls there is a beautiful palace. It contains rooms and halls built of carved marble, courtyards with fountains and pools of water, and a mosque where the emperor and his family went to worship. They lived in great comfort with hundreds of servants to look after them.

Crusaders returning home to Europe brought back many new ideas and objects that they had seen in Arab castles. Beautiful carpets, glass and metalwork decorated their chambers. They used spices in their food and wove clothes from rich silks. An Arabic instrument called an astrolabe helped European sailors navigate at sea. The numbers we use today were adapted from the Arabic system.

◁ This flask was made in Syria in 1250. The swirling 'arabesque' patterns were enamelled on glass by skilled Arab craftsmen.

THE END OF AN AGE

CLOUDS OF BLACK SMOKE roll out of the great hall's fireplace. A biting wind whistles through gaps in the windows and the candles splutter. The lord and his family sit shivering in thick woollen cloaks. They are fed up with living like this and want to move to a new, more comfortable home.

Kitchen

Look-out tower

Garderobe

Solar

Great hall

Chapel

Entrance hall

Stores

As the Middle Ages drew to a close, life became more peaceful. Lords no longer needed castles to defend their lands. Some tried to modify their strongholds, to make them more comfortable. Castles like Warkworth, in Northumberland, England, were transformed at great expense into luxurious homes. But gradually, many lords abandoned their cold, costly castles and left them to fall into ruins.

△ Warkworth Castle, in 1500. People no longer wanted to live in such powerful strongholds. They preferred more comfortable homes.

Some new castles were built in Europe in the nineteenth century. One of the most famous builders was King Ludwig II of Bavaria. These modern castles were designed for comfortable living, with large windows and luxury fittings. They were known as 'sham' castles, because they did not serve the real function of a castle. The lord and lady of a sham castle did not have to worry about defending it from enemy knights or controlling the peasants on their land.

▽ King Ludwig II built the 'fairy tale' castle of Neuschwanstein in Germany between 1869 and 1881.

TIMELINE

c. 950	c. 1020	1066	1086
The castle as the centre of feudal estates begins to appear.	In Persia, Avicenna writes the *Canon of Medicine*.	The Normans win the Battle of Hastings. After this date, the Normans build many castles across England.	The Domesday Book is compiled. It records a survey of all the lands in England.

1180	c. 1278	1283	1291
The first written reference is made to a windmill in Europe.	Leeds Castle becomes a royal palace.	King Edward I begins to build Conway and other castles after his conquest of Wales.	Crusaders called the Knights of the Order of St John make a base at Kolossi Castle, Cyprus, after suffering defeats in the Holy Land.

1387-1400	c.1400		c.1450
English poet Geoffrey Chaucer writes his poem about pilgrims, called the *Canterbury Tales*.	More castles have fireplaces with chimneys and private apartments.		German printer Johan Gutenberg invents a printing press. Books help to spread learning. Castle life is at its peak in Japan.

1095	c. 1150	c. 1170	c. 1180
Pope Urban II calls on Christian knights in Europe to make the First Crusade to the holy city of Jerusalem.	Castelnau Castle is built in France.	King Henry II rebuilds the castle at Scarborough, in England.	King Henry II orders Dover Castle to be rebuilt, which takes many years.

1300s	1300s	1347-9	1370-1400
Bagpipes are played in many countries.	Many castles now have private chambers for the lord and lady, such as the solar.	A plague called the Black Death kills over one-third of Europe's population.	Jean de Froissart writes his *Chronicles of France and England*. They describe castle life at this time.

c.1500	1628-66	1869-81	
Castle life begins to decline in most of Europe.	The reign of Emperor Shah Jahan, who completes the building of the Red Fort.	The sham castle of Neuschwanstein is built in Germany.	

GLOSSARY

Anvil A block on which metal is hammered by a blacksmith.

Barter Exchange goods.

Besieged Surrounded by enemy forces, and cut off from supplies.

Chastise To punish or beat someone.

Coat of arms The badge of a nobleman.

Crusade A holy war, particularly one fought by Christians against Muslims in the Middle East.

Formidable Causing fear.

Garret Top floor or attic.

Garrison The soldiers who are stationed in a castle.

Gatehouse A building at the entrance to a castle.

Knight A nobleman who receives land in return for military service.

Latin A language spoken widely in Europe in the Middle Ages.

Litters Enclosed carriages carried by men or horses.

Loggia An open-sided gallery.

Lute A medieval stringed instrument.

Manuscript A hand-written book.

Middle East Lands of south-west Asia, and northern Africa, dominated by Muslim peoples.

Minstrel A medieval singer or musician.

Moat A deep, wide ditch surrounding a castle's walls, often filled with water.

Mosque The place of worship for the Muslim religion.

Muslim A member of the Islamic religion followed by many people in the Middle East.

Noble An important person, usually with a title such as baron, count or duke, who held land in return for services to the king or queen.

Pages Boys in training to be knights.

Peasants People of low social class who work on the land.

Pedlars Travelling sellers of goods.

Pilgrim Someone who makes a journey to a holy place.

Pope The leader of the Christian Church in Western Europe.

Pottage A thick soup or stew made from vegetables.

Samurai A Japanese warrior, similar to a European knight.

Seal An engraved design on a ring or stamp, pressed into hot wax as a means of identification on documents.

Squire A knight's servant.

Steward The man responsible for running the lord's business.

Stonemasons People who prepare and carve stone for building.

Wet-nurses Women employed to nurse and suckle someone else's child.

FURTHER INFORMATION

PLACES TO VISIT

Chirk Castle, Clwyd, Wales
Chirk Castle is set in a beautiful estate in the Welsh countryside.

Dover Castle, Kent
Dover Castle has a deep well from which water was pumped up to different rooms.

Leeds Castle, Kent
The spectacular thirteenth-century buildings of this castle survive.

Scarborough Castle, North Yorkshire
This castle was originally a Viking stronghold, and was rebuilt by Henry II in 1170.

Tower of London, London
You can visit the royal St John's Chapel in the Tower.

Warkworth Castle, Northumberland
This was one of the most important strongholds in the north of England.

BOOKS

Best Ever Book of Castles
    by P. Steele (Kingfisher, 1997)
Castle by C. Gravett
    (Dorling Kindersley, 2002)
Medieval Life by A. Langley
    (Dorling Kindersley, 2002)
The Royal Castle by J. Farndon
    (Viking Children's Books, 1997)
Scottish Castles Through History
    by R. Dargie (Wayland, 1998)

INDEX